978-1-5359-4338-3

Published by B&H Publishing Group
Nashville, Tennessee

Author is represented by the literary agency of
The Fedd Agency, Inc. Post Office Box 341973, Austin, TX 78734.

Cover photography by Micah Kandros

Unless otherwise noted, all Scripture quotations are
taken from the Christian Standard Bible®, copyright
© 2017 by Holman Bible Publishers. Used by permission.
Christian Standard Bible® and CSB® are federally registered
trademarks of Holman Bible Publishers.

1 2 3 4 5 6 7 • 22 21 20 19 18

PLAYING
FOR MORE

PLAYING FOR MORE

CASE
KEENUM

with TAYLOR COMBS

PUBLISHING GROUP

NASHVILLE, TENNESSEE

Contents

Introduction

PREPARATION. We prepare for the most important things in life. We prepare to speak in public. We prepare before the big job interview. We prepare for the big game.

For most of us, in our most honest moments, we would say that we want the most out of life—every single day (I know I do!). So every day counts, and there are no off-days when you are pursuing life to the fullest.

So, why don't we prepare for each and every day like it's "the big day"?

There's no good answer to this question, but we all have excuses:

"I'm just too busy."
"I need my sleep!"
"Time got away from me."

None of us are perfect, but we all want what's best—that's the dilemma. When we pursue life to the fullest, we can't do it on our own strength, and so we need to turn our attention to the only One who has ever modeled this type of life: Jesus Christ.

The devotional you hold in your hands is intended to be a playbook for your life. The challenge is simple: spend 30 days preparing for whatever circumstances lay ahead.

The Bible is full of wisdom that is necessary and sufficient for abundant life. Each day begins with Scripture and encouragement that has helped me, so far, on life's journey. I hope it will do the same for you.

A personal relationship with Jesus not only requires listening to Him in His Word, but also time spent in prayer. Prayer, alone, doesn't have to be formal or flowery. In fact, Jesus said that's the exact wrong way to pray (Matthew 6:5)! Prayer is simply talking to your Father in heaven. End each day in this devotional like this: "Father, I love You because You are _____. I confess that I _____. Will You forgive me for these sins? Thank You for _____. Father, I need Your help with _____. Help me to see Your plan for me today, and love those You've put in my path. Amen."

I can't promise you will have it all together at the end of 30 days, but I can promise that you won't be the same either. Becoming more and more like Jesus is a process. Take your first step today, and trust the process.

—Case Keenum

John 3:16

For God loved the world in this way: He gave his one and only Son, so that everyone who believes in him will not perish but have eternal life.

Day 1

How do you know somebody loves you? I mean, how do you *really* know?

The night that I proposed to Kimberly, I tried to make it crystal clear that I loved her with all my heart. I had to be smart about the proposal. I wanted to surprise Kimberly, but she's got these secret ninja detective skills. Seriously, she finds out everything. Pulling off this surprise was not going to be easy.

Eventually, I worked out a plan. I took her to a nice dinner and on the way out, I slyly said, "Hey, let's stop by the stadium and see if we can get in." And the gate to the Houston Cougars' stadium just happened to be conveniently unlocked.

When we walked in, she immediately saw a row of candles that stretched from the end zone to the 50-yard line, leading to a table covered in rose petals at mid-field. I got down on one knee and popped the question—and she said yes! Immediately, both of our families (who had been hiding in the press box) went wild cheering. Music started playing. We were starting the rest of our lives together . . . and I think I made it clear that I *really* loved her.

But no one can ever top what God did to show us that He loves us.

The Bible tells us that all people are sinners and have turned away from God. There must be a just punishment for our sin. So how can we be forgiven? Here's the amazing thing: God sent His Son to the earth to take our punishment, to trade places with us.

Jesus Christ is the Son of God. He is fully human and fully God (crazy, right?). Even though we have all sinned, Jesus never sinned. He lived a perfect life. And because He lived a perfect life, He was able to trade places with us. He went to the cross and took the punishment of God for our sins on Himself, and if we believe in Him, our sins will be forgiven. Not only that, but God will see us as perfectly righteous—clean and spotless, without any hint of sin—because the righteousness of Jesus is counted to us.

I really love my wife a lot, and I try to do a lot to prove it. But no one has proved their love as clearly as God did for us. As we start into this journey, can I encourage you to think about how much God loves you? Have you accepted that love yet? Have you received it? Jesus says if you believe in Him, you will be forgiven and will have eternal life.

Use the space below to respond to God
by writing a prayer to Him.

_____

_____

_____

_____

_____

_____

_____

_____

_____

_____

_____

_____

_____

_____

_____

_____

_____

_____

_____

Isaiah 40:28-31

Do you not know? Have you not heard? The LORD is the everlasting God, the Creator of the whole earth. He never becomes faint or weary; there is no limit to his understanding. He gives strength to the faint and strengthens the powerless. Youths may become faint and weary, and young men stumble and fall, but those who trust in the LORD will renew their strength; they will soar on wings like eagles; they will run and not become weary, they will walk and not faint.

Day 2

FOX sideline reporter Chris Myers seemed surprised. I imagine lots of people watching were surprised as well. When asked where the Minnesota Miracle ranked among the best moments of my life, there was only one honest answer: third.

Marrying my wife Kimberly, without a doubt, comes in second. If you knew her, you'd understand how marrying her is better than anything football has to offer.

But what takes first place? The greatest moment of my life was accepting Jesus Christ as my Lord and Savior. That moment was a game-changer. Nothing will ever take its place as the greatest moment of my life.

You see, I'm not a football player who happens to be a Christian; I'm a Christian who happens to be a football player. I don't live and die by my successes or failures on the field, because I'm not ultimately defined by them. My hope is in something much better and much more certain than touchdowns, completion percentages, trophies, or record books.

Playing for more starts with hoping for more. If your ultimate hope in life is a state championship, a college scholarship, hearing your name called on draft day, or winning a Super Bowl, you'll never be truly fulfilled—even if you get those things. But when you place your hope—your trust—in the Lord, you receive a promise, a promise that He will renew your strength, and that you will soar on wings like eagles.

This isn't a promise about increasing your bench press or your 40-time. It's a promise of heaven. A promise of endless life in the presence of God, with renewed strength. When your hope is in the Lord and you know that He will renew your strength, you can make it through the ups and downs of life—on and off the field—and still be fulfilled.

The funny thing is, the times in my life when my focus, energy, and trust have been most centered in God and my relationship with Him have been the times when I have succeeded most on the field. It's like placing your hope in a sure thing instead of the things of this world, which takes the pressure off, and frees you up to perform more to your potential.

Regardless of where you are in life, whether you're experiencing success or struggle, whether your focus is on the gridiron, in the classroom, at home, or at the workplace, put your hope in the Lord. Success in this life comes and goes, but "those who trust in the Lord will renew their strength."

Use the space below to respond to God
by writing a prayer to Him.

_____

_____

_____

_____

_____

_____

_____

_____

_____

_____

_____

_____

_____

_____

_____

_____

_____

_____

_____

Proverbs 19:21

Many plans are in a person's heart, but the LORD's decree will prevail.

Day 3

I've got to be honest with you: I would not have chosen the route to get to where I am.

If you had told me when I was fourteen that I'd be the starting quarterback for the Broncos at age thirty, it would've almost been too good to be true. I would've been through the roof with excitement. But here's probably how I would think the journey would go:

Age 16: Ranked as a 5-star quarterback
Age 17: Raking in offers from every major college football program
Age 18: Head off to perennial top 10 team
Age 19: Named a starter in the Big-12 as a true freshman
Age 22: Heisman trophy winner; selected in the first round of the draft
Age 23–30: Starting quarterback in Denver; make the playoffs every year

But in reality, my journey has been just a little different . . .

Age 16: Ranked as a 2-star quarterback

Age 17: Receive one offer to play college football for the Houston Cougars

Age 18: Head off to the University of Houston

Age 19: Redshirt

Age 20–22: Starting quarterback

Age 23: Tear ACL

Age 24: Sixth year of eligibility to play for Houston; undrafted; sign with the Texans

Age 24–28: Bounce around the League; start some games; win some games; lose some games

Age 29: Sign with the Minnesota Vikings; make the playoffs; Minneapolis Miracle

Age 30: Sign with the Denver Broncos

Yeah, it's safe to say I took a pretty winding route. But you know what? That's okay! The Bible says that we make lots of plans, but God's plans are the ones that come to pass. And that's a good thing. If I were wise enough and powerful enough to create a whole universe and everything in it, I guess it would be good for my plans to come to pass. But in the mean time, I'll trust God's. And whatever path you're on right now, I hope you'll do the same.

Use the space below to respond to God
by writing a prayer to Him.

_____

_____

_____

_____

_____

_____

_____

_____

_____

_____

_____

_____

_____

_____

_____

_____

_____

_____

_____

_____

Romans 12:1-2

Therefore, brothers and sisters, in view of the mercies of God, I urge you to present your bodies as a living sacrifice, holy and pleasing to God; this is your true worship. Do not be conformed to this age, but be transformed by the renewing of your mind, so that you may discern what is the good, pleasing, and perfect will of God.

Day 4

It was a weird living situation. Me, my girlfriend, and my mom. I don't recommend it.

But Kimberly—now my wife—and I had decided a long time ago that we were waiting for marriage, so moving in wasn't an option. But after I went down with an ACL tear, I needed full-time care. So the two women closest to me were all hands on deck. Me, my girlfriend, and my mom. We had a bed, a couch, and an air mattress—what more could we need?

Like I said, this was a weird living situation. But being transformed by the renewing of our minds, and not being conformed to the world around us, means followers of Jesus do weird things. Because of a decision we had made to honor God and obey Him, we had to take extra precautions, and the result was something that looked a lot different from the world.

How often in life are we tempted to think that if we just allowed ourselves to give in to the pressure of those around us, things would be easier? Maybe it's the pressure to gossip with coworkers about other coworkers. Maybe it's the temptation to sleep in instead of going to church. Maybe all your friends are going to *that* party. In all of these instances, wouldn't it just be easier to give in?

But when we follow Jesus, the Bible tells us that He make us new. When He makes us new, He begins renewing our minds, so that we see, experience, and think about things—all things—in a new way. We now do everything for a new reason, with a new purpose.

All that we do as followers of Christ is meant to glorify Him. When I lace up my clean cleats and run through the tunnel on game day, it's easy to think it's all about me. I need to be focused on my stats, my completion percentage, the number of touchdowns I throw, and what the commentators are saying about me after the game is over. But being transformed by the renewing of my mind means that when I take the field, I'm doing it in a new light—in the light of glorying God.

The same is true for you. I don't know where you are in life, but I do know that God gives a new meaning and purpose to whatever tasks He has assigned you. As you go to your workplace, study for tests, mow the lawn, hang out with your friends, introduce yourself to your neighbors, and even watch football games, He has called you to do so in a new way—in a way that glorifies Him.

Use the space below to respond to God
by writing a prayer to Him.

Psalm 8:1

LORD, our Lord, how magnificent is your name throughout the earth! You have covered the heavens with your majesty.

Day 5

Who are some of your favorite athletes?

Growing up in Texas, Troy Aikman was the man. He was my favorite player on my favorite team. I loved watching him play. John Elway was another one. You don't talk about great quarterbacks without mentioning his name. (By the way, it's pretty cool that now I get to play for Denver, where he is the general manager!) When I got a little older, I started watching Drew Brees a lot. Drew is an amazing quarterback and an even better dude.

Sometimes, just hearing the name of someone you admire can put goose bumps on your arms. You hear their name and the adjectives start flowing out— *awesome, amazing, the best, the GOAT.*

The Bible talks about God's name like this. It says His name is *magnificent.*

As awesome as our heroes are, no one is like God. It's cool to throw some touchdown passes and win a Super Bowl or two, but God literally created the universe. He spoke it into existence out of nothing. He is sovereign over all of His creation now. Nothing happens without His oversight and will.

The question is, how often do we stop and think about how magnificent the name of God is? Sometimes, we get so caught up in the shiny little things in front of us that we miss the amazing thing that should be grabbing our attention. Like staring at a flickering candle while fireworks go off in the background. Or reading a text on your phone while a playoff game is in overtime. We're tempted to do the same with God—to get distracted by something pretty cool when the most amazing thing ever is happening right in front of us.

The best thing in the world for us is to get to know God, to learn more about Him, and to think about how amazing He truly is. But we have to be disciplined to do this. We have to be intentional, or we'll keep getting distracted by less important, less impressive things. One way to do this is to spend time reading His Word in the Bible and praying. Another way is to become a member of a church so you can hear other people talking about what God has done in their lives, sing together of how great He is, and hear preaching from the Bible. If you're not already doing these things, what are you waiting on? Don't get distracted by the little trifles of this life . . . the God of the universe is the only thing that is truly magnificent.

Use the space below to respond to God
by writing a prayer to Him.

_____

_____

_____

_____

_____

_____

_____

_____

_____

_____

_____

_____

_____

_____

_____

_____

_____

_____

_____

_____

_____

Colossians 1:16

For everything was created by him, in heaven and on earth, the visible and the invisible, whether thrones or dominions or rulers or authorities—all things have been created through him and for him.

Day 6

How do you define yourself? When you introduce yourself to someone you're just meeting, what kinds of things do you tell them? Maybe you talk about your job, your family, or your hobbies. Maybe you tell them what school you go to or what you like to do with your friends.

Another way of asking this question is, *What is your core identity?*

We find our identity in all kinds of places. We look to our jobs, our marriage (or singleness), our children (or lack thereof), and even the number of people who follow us on social media for our identity. I often tell people that I'm not a football player who happens to be a Christian, I'm a Christian who happens to play football. This is saying something about my identity. One day, I'll no longer be a football player. If I make it to age forty on the gridiron, that will be a great, long career. But what happens when I turn forty-one? Or fifty? Or eighty? You can bet I'll be tossing the pigskin with my kids and grandkids, but I certainly won't be taking hits from linebackers at sixty-five! And if I see my identity primarily as a football player, then I'll feel lost and incomplete when the day comes that I'm no longer running through that tunnel to take the field.

Fundamentally, playing football is just what I *do*. Being a Christian is who I *am*. And that will never change. No matter what I'm doing, I will always be a Christian. That's my identity.

And when you understand that your identity is fundamentally about being a Christian, it reshapes everything else. Playing football is not who I am; it's what I do. But when I understand my identity as a Christian, it totally changes the way I play football! Understanding who I am gives new meaning to what I do.

The Bible says that all things were created by Jesus, through Jesus, and for Jesus. You know what's included in all things? Football. That's right, even football was created by Jesus and for His glory. So when I understand my identity primarily as a Christian, then I can begin to do what I do for the reason I was created—to give glory to Jesus. Whether I win or lose, whether I retire at thirty-two or forty-two, and whatever the future may hold, I will always seek to do whatever I do for the glory of God.

You're not primarily a husband, father, football player, basketball player, student, or friend. You're primarily a Christian. And when you understand that, you can begin to do all those things for the glory of the One who created them.

Use the space below to respond to God
by writing a prayer to Him.

_____

_____

_____

_____

_____

_____

_____

_____

_____

_____

_____

_____

_____

_____

_____

_____

_____

_____

_____

Psalm 16:11

You reveal the path of life to me; in your presence is abundant joy; at your right hand are eternal pleasures.

Day 7

What's the best thing you can possibly imagine happening in your life? What achievement at work or at school would change everything for you? What's the one thing you're constantly thinking about or dreaming about that would make your life all you could hope for?

After the Minneapolis Miracle, I think a lot of people assumed, "This is the one thing Case Keenum needed to totally change his life." That's probably why I was asked in the post-game interview, "Is this the best moment of your life?" Don't get me wrong—the Minneapolis Miracle was *awesome*. Winning a playoff game, doing it the way we did it, and having my brothers on the team and my friends and family on the sidelines to celebrate with—it was an amazing moment. But it wasn't the best moment of my life.

The best moment of my life was meeting my Lord and Savior Jesus Christ. Here's the thing: God gives us great moments in life to celebrate, to have fun, and to experience real joy. But the only place we can find "abundant joy" is, according to Psalm 16, in His presence. The only place we can get "eternal pleasures" is at His right hand.

I don't know what you think you want more than anything else, but I can tell you what you need more than anything else: the presence of God. This is what we were all made for. Not just for achievements that feel really important at the time but will probably be forgotten a generation from now (if not sooner!). We're created for joy that lasts forever, because we have a God who lasts forever.

Many people have said that we are created with a God-sized hole in our hearts, and until He fills that hole, we won't really be satisfied. Last-second playoff victories, promotions at work, good friendships—all these things are gifts from God that give us joy. But they can't fill up that God-sized hole in our hearts. He's the only one who can fill it.

What are you trying to put into that God-sized hole? If you're still looking for the best moment of your life somewhere else, take my word for it: you'll only find it in Him.

Use the space below to respond to God
by writing a prayer to Him.

_____

_____

_____

_____

_____

_____

_____

_____

_____

_____

_____

_____

_____

_____

_____

_____

_____

_____

_____

_____

Joshua 1:9

Haven't I commanded you: be strong and coura-geous? Do not be afraid or discouraged, for the LORD your God is with you wherever you go.

Day 8

Football takes some guts. Sure, that's true of other sports as well, but *man* do you get hit hard playing football! Whether you're a wide receiver running crossing routes, a quarterback being chased by a massive defensive lineman, or a punter when the offensive line breaks down, you've got to really have some courage.

That's not only true for football, it's true about every good thing in life. Nothing good comes easy, as the old saying goes, and it's true. Whether it's school or relationships or marriage or work, you've got to have some courage to accomplish something. Courage to have tough conversations. Courage to keep grinding when people are doubting you. Courage to keep walking when tragedy hits. But how do you get that courage? Do we just muster it up on our own?

In the Old Testament book of Joshua, God's people are about to enter the Promised Land. God had promised this land to His people generations ago; and after years and years of waiting, the moment was finally at hand. But they were going to have to have some courage, because it was going to take a battle. Actually, it was going to take lots of battles. So what did God tell them? He told them to have courage *because He would be with them*. This is the best way—the only way, really—to have courage.

We can try all we want to find courage from other sources than this. I can try to have courage because I'm good enough or strong enough or talented enough. I can try to get courage from other people saying nice things about me. But ultimately, those sources of courage will run out, and I'll be back at square one.

As much as I need courage on the football field, it's not the place I need courage the most. The biggest need for courage in my life is so I can follow Jesus. Jesus takes us to difficult places. He asks a lot of us. He gets us out of our comfort zone. We can only really be obedient to what He is calling us to do when we take our focus off ourselves and put it on God—He is with us wherever we go.

Interestingly, Jesus says something similar in the New Testament to what this verse in Joshua says. As Jesus is giving His closing command to His followers, the command to make disciples of the whole world, He says, "I am with you always." We have nothing to fear, because the God who created us, the Savior who died for us, is always with us.

Use the space below to respond to God
by writing a prayer to Him.

_____

_____

_____

_____

_____

_____

_____

_____

_____

_____

_____

_____

_____

_____

_____

_____

_____

_____

_____

_____

_____

Ecclesiastes 4:9-12

Two are better than one because they have a good reward for their efforts. For if either falls, his companion can lift him up; but pity the one who falls without another to lift him up. Also, if two lie down together, they can keep warm; but how can one person alone keep warm? And if someone overpowers one person, two can resist him. A cord of three strands is not easily broken.

Day 9

You know who doesn't get enough love from football fans? Offensive linemen. Seriously. Nothing happens without those guys. Want to have a successful running attack? Got to have great linemen to open up holes. Want to have a great passing attack? Got to have some big dudes who can protect your quarterback.

That's the thing about football. Unless you have a whole team working together, you can't win. On offense, unless your line, backs, receivers, and quarterback are doing their job and looking out for each other, it's going to be really hard to put up any points.

The same thing is true about life. Ecclesiastes—written by a guy named Solomon, who the Bible says was the wisest person in history—says, "Two are better than one because they have a good reward for their efforts" (4:9), and, "A cord of three strands is not easily broken" (4:12). If we try to live our lives alone, without the support and accountability of others, we will fail time and time again. But if we live connected to the people God has given us, who are moving in the same direction in life, we'll fair much better.

For me, this has always been my family. My mom and dad have always been there to support me and encourage me, to pick me up when I get down.

In college, it was often the team chaplain Mikado. That guy always had my back, but also knew how to cut straight with me when I was acting like a dummy!

Now, of course, the number one person in my life who is there for everything I do is my wife Kimberly. Kimberly and I don't make any decisions alone. We're always praying for and with each other, encouraging each other, and helping each other through whatever life throws our way. Seriously, I have no idea where I'd be if not for Kimberly.

So who is your offensive line? Who are the people in your life who are always keeping you on the right track? The people who pray for you and speak wisdom into your life right when you need it? If you have those people, great! Lean into those relationships. If not, keep your head on a swivel for who they might be, and pray that God would bring great friends and mentors into your life to keep you pointed in the right direction.

Use the space below to respond to God
by writing a prayer to Him.

_____

_____

_____

_____

_____

_____

_____

_____

_____

_____

_____

_____

_____

_____

_____

_____

_____

_____

_____

_____

_____

Ephesians 6:10-13

Finally, be strengthened by the Lord and by his vast strength. Put on the full armor of God so that you can stand against the schemes of the devil. For our struggle is not against flesh and blood, but against the rulers, against the authorities, against the cosmic powers of this darkness, against evil, spiritual forces in the heavens. For this reason take up the full armor of God, so that you may be able to resist in the evil day, and having prepared everything, to take your stand.

Day 10

Football is a physical sport. People get injured all the time, and I've certainly had my fair share of injuries. The worst was when I tore my ACL my senior year at Houston.

Dudes fly around out there on the football field. Big dudes. Linebackers and defensive ends are always chasing me down. Safeties and cornerbacks are always trying to take out my receivers. You've got to keep your head on a swivel or you'll find yourself on a cart heading for the locker room in no time.

Given how easy it is to get injured in football, imagine how foolish I would have to be to take the field without my gear. No helmet, no shoulder pads, no cleats. I'd be hurt in seconds!

If we agree it would be foolish to walk onto the field without any gear, why do we sometimes live like we can walk into life without any gear?

The Bible calls this gear the armor of God, and it makes very clear that we desperately need it if we want any chance at success.

Just like I have linebackers and defensive lineman trying to chase me down, the Bible says the devil is trying to chase us down. Everywhere we turn, he wants us to slip up. How can we win the game? By suiting up.

We need to wear truth—the truth God has revealed in His Word—like a belt around our waist, holding everything in our lives together.

We need the righteousness God gives us in Christ on our chests, guarding our hearts.

We need readiness on our feet like sandals, so that we can share the good news at a moment's notice.

We need the shield of faith to protect us from all of Satan's attacks.

We need the helmet of salvation and the sword of the Spirit for protection.

When we face temptation to sin, discouragement, anxiety, fear, or doubt, if we're not suited up with the armor of God, we'll be in big trouble. Like me running onto the field helmetless and barefoot, it won't be pretty. In all these things, we need to be ready.

Use the space below to respond to God
by writing a prayer to Him.

_____

_____

_____

_____

_____

_____

_____

_____

_____

_____

_____

_____

_____

_____

_____

_____

_____

_____

_____

_____

Proverbs 12:15

A fool's way is right in his own eyes, but whoever listens to counsel is wise.

Day 11

I was a pretty good kid growing up, but like all teen-agers, I managed to get in a little trouble every now and then. Especially if it involved competition. If somebody told me I couldn't do something, or couldn't do it as well as them, you could bet I would be out to prove them wrong.

So this one time at a high school football game, while the band was doing their thing, one of my teammates bet me I couldn't throw an ice cube into a tuba. No, you didn't read that wrong. And yes, I went for it. My competitive side got the best of me . . . and I *nailed* it.

But as you might imagine, my old man was not too happy about this incident. I'm pretty sure I spent several weeks doing some kind of mandatory labor to make up for the ol' ice-in-the-tuba trick!

At the time, I was probably pretty annoyed at my dad. I thought it was a harmless trick and didn't see what the big deal was. But he saw it differently, and he was right.

I can see now what an immature move that was, and how it probably really hurt the feelings of the kid playing the tuba. And if I had listened to the wisdom that my mom and dad poured into me in my childhood, I never would have done something like that.

The Bible says that people who don't listen to counsel are fools. People who aren't willing to accept the wisdom of their parents—like me during some parts of my childhood years—are acting like fools. People who ignore their coaches, their teachers, their mentors, and others who know what's best for them and want what's best for them . . . you guessed it. Fools.

Sometimes it can be hard to take advice from older, wiser people, but God's Word says it's worth it. He says it's wise to listen to counsel, and we should certainly work to become wise people.

Whose counsel are you listening to? Are you listening to the good and wise counsel of godly friends, parents, pastors, mentors, and leaders in your life? Or are you trying to fly solo and do it on your own? Don't be foolish. Find good counsel, learn from it, and apply it to your life.

Use the space below to respond to God
by writing a prayer to Him.

Matthew 7:13-14

Enter through the narrow gate. For the gate is wide and the road broad that leads to destruction, and there are many who go through it. How narrow is the gate and difficult the road that leads to life, and few find it.

Day 12

As a football player, I naturally love movies about football. One of my favorites is the 2000 classic *Remember the Titans*. Denzel makes the perfect ball coach, and it's such an inspiring film.

At one point in the movie, Coach Boone (Denzel) makes a speech where he makes clear what his definition of success is: perfection. "You miss a block, you run a mile!" At the end of the movie, he softens up a bit and starts to ease off from his original demands, until one of his star players—Julius, a defensive end—reminds him of that measure of success.

What is your definition of success? How do you define it?

The world measures success by fame, praise, material possessions, and a whole bunch of other things that really aren't that lasting and aren't that fulfilling. But this desire for worldly things is what the Bible calls the "wide road"—and that road doesn't lead anywhere good. Sometimes, unfortunately, people view Christianity as something they can add to their life to help them reach their measure of success. "If I make this much money, have this job, throw this many touchdown passes, win this many games, marry this person, and *mix* in a little bit of Jesus, I'll be successful.

But that's not at all how Christianity works. Christianity isn't about helping you be successful on your own terms; it's about living a life with and for Jesus, so that He changes your definition of success. It's about following Him on the "narrow road."

It's been true in my life that when I've been focused on Jesus, I've performed better on the football field. But it's not like I have to behave well for God to make me successful. Honestly, I think I've performed best in those moments because knowing that God has everything under control just takes the pressure off. I can loosen up and have some fun!

Thing is, even if I fail miserably on the football field, I can still be successful. On the flip side, I can have a really great football career, but be unsuccessful at what matters most. Sounds weird, right? But living for Jesus doesn't help you achieve your own definition of success; if you give your life to Christ, He gives you a whole new definition of success.

There are a lot of ways people define success, but here's my definition: living *with* and *for* Christ. If you've got those down, regardless of everything else, you're living a truly successful life.

Use the space below to respond to God
by writing a prayer to Him.

Colossians 3:12-14

Therefore, as God's chosen ones, holy and dearly loved, put on compassion, kindness, humility, gentleness, and patience, bearing with one another and forgiving one another if anyone has a grievance against another. Just as the Lord has forgiven you, so you are also to forgive. Above all, put on love, which is the perfect bond of unity.

Day 13

Before every game I play, my dad sends me some version of the following text:

Pray hard. Play hard. Take care of the football. Have fun.

It's like a little to-do list with the most important things I need for each game. First, I need to pray hard. Not just that I'll win or have a good game, but that I'll represent Him well on the field. Jesus is the most important thing about my life, and if I'm playing football without considering Him, I'm missing the boat.

I also have to play hard. No matter what the score is—we could be down 50–0—being a person of character and integrity means continuing to play hard.

Quarterbacks touch the ball more on offense than any other player. If there's one thing we have to do, it's to take care of the football. No lazy passes. No trying to squeeze the ball into nonexistent windows or make impossible passes. Take. Care. Of. The. Football.

Lastly, you gotta have fun. If I can't have fun out there, what's the point? I'm living my childhood dream, for crying out loud!

In Colossians 3, Paul gives a sort of to-do list text like this to the Colossian church. Kind of like this:

Be kind and compassionate. Stay humble. Be gentle and patient. And don't forget to love.

Paul gives the believers a list of the most important things—the things they can never forget to do. And the last one, for Paul, is the most important. "Above all," he says, "put on love, which is the perfect bond of unity." Love isn't just the most important of all the reminders Paul sends the believers; it's the one that binds them all together.

Are you living by this checklist? As we strive to be more and more like Jesus, this is a pretty helpful list to follow. Jesus was kind, compassionate, humble, gentle, patient, and forgiving to us. And above all, He loves us, which binds together all the others. Let's go do the same for the people around us.

Use the space below to respond to God
by writing a prayer to Him.

_____

_____

_____

_____

_____

_____

_____

_____

_____

_____

_____

_____

_____

_____

_____

_____

_____

_____

_____

_____

_____

_____

2 Corinthians 5:17

Therefore, if anyone is in Christ, he is a new creation; the old has passed away, and see, the new has come!

Day 14

When I was a senior at the University of Houston, in the third game of the season, I tore my ACL. I was down for the count. The recovery process was excruciating. Meds that made me sick to my stomach. Physical therapy that hurt so bad I could hardly push through. And worse than that, the anguish of having to watch my team play without me, and of not knowing whether I'd ever get another shot.

After going through the whole recovery process, I was back. I was physically ready to go. Then when I found out I would be allowed to play for one more year due to my injury, I was *really* ready to go. I felt like a new man.

God's Word tells us that something similar happens when we become Christians. The big story of the Bible is one of creation, the fall, and new creation. God created everything good, but because Adam and Eve, the first humans, sinned, the creation was broken. This is called "the fall." But God didn't just give up on His plan. He responded by beginning a new creation. In fact, this new creation was His plan all along.

God the Father sent Jesus the Son to Earth to start this process of new creation. When Jesus comes back to Earth, He will complete it. The whole world will be made new. It will be good, with no more sin or sickness or sadness.

But in the mean time, He is starting with us. God is making new creations out of us.

Every person who believes in Jesus becomes a new creation—a new man (or woman!), to use the language I used above. The old sinful self passes away, and God gives us a new heart, a heart that believes in Jesus and wants to follow Him.

But here's the hard part of the Christian life. Once we've been made a new creation, the old creation still tries to rear its ugly head. Just like I've had to take good care of my knee since tearing my ACL to keep from reinjuring it, we have to take care to follow Jesus, to keep becoming the new creation that He's making us into.

Have you been made new by Jesus? If not, believe in Him, and He will make you new! If you have been made new by Him, examine your life. What parts still look like the old you? Ask Jesus to change those parts of your life to make you more and more like Him.

Use the space below to respond to God
by writing a prayer to Him.

_____

_____

_____

_____

_____

_____

_____

_____

_____

_____

_____

_____

_____

_____

_____

_____

_____

_____

_____

_____

_____

Matthew 6:25-27

Therefore I tell you: Don't worry about your life, what you will eat or what you will drink; or about your body, what you will wear. Isn't life more than food and the body more than clothing? Consider the birds of the sky: They don't sow or reap or gather into barns, yet your heavenly Father feeds them. Aren't you worth more than they? Can any of you add one moment to his life span by worrying?

Day 15

At times during my career I've pressed too hard. Do you know that feeling? After redshirting my first year at Houston, I started to press too hard as a redshirt freshman. I wanted more than anything to be named the starter. I pushed and pushed and pushed, but at some point, I had to step back and ask the question, "Are you having any fun?"

A similar thing happened when I first got to the league. Trying to make the roster. Trying to earn a starting spot. Those same old feelings of worry and anxiety crept back in. And feelings like that can take over.

Whether we're worrying about school, work, relationships, or just life in general, worry tends to take over. But here's the thing: We start worrying when we think we're in control. But Jesus tells us that our worry can't add a single hair to our head. It can't add a single day to our lives. As much as we worry, we're really not the ones in control.

Surprisingly, the Bible says that's good news. Why is it good news? Because God is the One in control. And He is not powerless to add hairs to our head or days to our lives; He is powerful enough to do anything He wants.

Not only is God powerful enough to do what He wants, He's also good, and He has promised to work for our good. The Bible tells us He is a good Father and He knows everything we need. We don't have to worry because we have a good, loving, powerful Father who cares for us and who is in control.

It may not be what you expect, but the times in my life when I've played the best football are the times when I've stopped pushing so hard. When I just relax and trust God to work out all the details, I not only play better, but I have more fun too!

So where do you need to relax and have a little fun? Where would your life be better if you just stopped pushing so hard and decided to trust God to work out all the details? Give it a try . . . I bet things will get better *and* you'll be able to lighten up and have some fun.

Use the space below to respond to God
by writing a prayer to Him.

_____

_____

_____

_____

_____

_____

_____

_____

_____

_____

_____

_____

_____

_____

_____

_____

_____

_____

_____

_____

_____

1 Samuel 16:7

But the LORD said to Samuel, "Do not look at his appearance or his stature because I have rejected him. Humans do not see what the LORD sees, for humans see what is visible, but the LORD sees the heart.

Day 16

Ever since high school, people have doubted me. *Not tall enough. Not big enough. Doesn't have the arm strength.* Coming out of high school, I was a two-star recruit. Coaches evaluated me on the externals, and they didn't always like what they saw.

Then I played for the University of Houston and, after finishing, entered the NFL Draft. What did I hear? More doubts. *Is he too short? Can he throw the deep ball?* I waited to hear my name called, but all I heard, pick after pick, round after round, were a bunch of people not named Case Keenum.

In all these seasons of life, I was judged on the externals. And this is how people naturally judge. We size people up from the outside. From what we can see. But God judges differently.

When God told His prophet Samuel to go anoint the next king for God's people, Samuel thought he was looking for a tall guy. A strong guy. An oldest sibling. But the man—well, the boy—that God led him to was the youngest of eight, and not even his father or his brothers thought he might be the king.

God made it very clear to Samuel, and to us, that He doesn't judge in the same way people do. We look at the externals, but God looks at our hearts.

This should tell us two things. First, we shouldn't let the doubters get to us. Whatever you do in life, if it's your aim to be successful, you will have doubters. Critics. Teammates. Coaches. Coworkers. Bosses. Talking heads. They'll doubt whether you're enough, because they're looking at the outside. But when you know that God looks at the inside, you don't have to worry about these critics. Get things right with God, do all that you do for His glory, and know that no one else's opinion can change what's ultimately true about you.

Second, we should seek to see people as God sees people. If He looks not at appearances, but at the heart, we should do the same. We should be able to love people regardless of height, weight, physical attractiveness, strength, skin color, wealth, or anything else external. We look at the heart, and there we will find a fellow human being who God loves, and therefore, who we should also love.

Use the space below to respond to God
by writing a prayer to Him.

_____

_____

_____

_____

_____

_____

_____

_____

_____

_____

_____

_____

_____

_____

_____

_____

_____

_____

_____

_____

_____

Psalm 5:1-3

*Listen to my words, L*ORD*; consider my sighing. Pay attention to the sound of my cry, my King and my God, for I pray to you. In the morning, L*ORD *, you hear my voice; in the morning I plead my case to you and watch expectantly.*

Day 17

Ever had a bad day? Of course you have. We all have them. What about a bad week? Year?

Sometimes bad things happen to us. Sometimes bad things just pile up. It's like you can't do anything without something going horribly wrong.

One of the darkest seasons of my life was after I tore my ACL. My junior season, we won a lot of games, and our offense was really clicking. I was on pace to potentially break a bunch of passing records. And we were playing in one of the most famous environments in college football: at the Rose Bowl.

We fell behind early. I knew we could come back, but I wasn't patient. I tried to squeeze a pass into a window that was way too small. The defender read my eyes and picked off the pass. *Shoot!*

Now I'm mad. So what am I going to do? Well, I'm gonna tackle the guy who just picked me off! But he was bigger than me, and apparently faster too, so when he cut up the field and I tried to go with him, something went wrong. I fell to the turf . . . I knew it immediately. I tore my ACL.

I was out for the year and went into a tailspin. Would I ever play another game for the Cougars? Were my NFL dreams over? Add to it that the meds I had to take made me sick as a dog. I lost thirty pounds while I was injured (not good for a football player!). I was down and out.

But we can be encouraged even when we're down and out. How? Because God doesn't leave us. And in fact, it's sometimes in those moments that are so frustrating, so depressing, that He draws so close to us.

The authors of the Bible understood that we have difficult seasons. In Psalm 5, King David cries out to God during one of these difficult seasons. "Pay attention to the sound of my cry," he said. And then in verse 3, he says this line I love: "I plead my case to you and *watch expectantly.*"

David knew that God wasn't done with him. He knew his story wasn't over. So he cried out to God, he prayed for God to come to his rescue, and as he did, he watched expectantly.

Are you watching expectantly for the Lord? Do you believe He is going to do something with you and in you? Do you believe He isn't done with you? Keep watching. The Lord is near to us even when we're at our lowest.

Use the space below to respond to God
by writing a prayer to Him.

_____

_____

_____

_____

_____

_____

_____

_____

_____

_____

_____

_____

_____

_____

_____

_____

_____

_____

_____

_____

_____

_____

James 1:2-4

Consider it a great joy, my brothers and sisters, whenever you experience various trials, because you know that the testing of your faith produces endurance. And let endurance have its full effect, so that you may be mature and complete, lacking nothing.

Day 18

My first couple of years in the NFL were rough. Well, first of all, getting to the NFL in the first place was rough. I set almost every record imaginable while I was at Houston, so you might think I was a high draft pick when I moved on to the next level. Nope. I waited and waited to hear my name called in the Draft, and it never happened. I was undrafted.

After that, I was back and forth between the roster and the practice squad, and was cut three times from NFL teams before things finally got steady. I wish I could say I was full of joy and happiness and so much fun to be around during that time, but the truth is, it was a difficult season of life! Any time you work hard for something and it doesn't seem to be panning out, it's difficult to have joy.

It's amazing, then, what James tells us at the beginning of his New Testament letter: "Consider it great joy . . . whenever you experience various trials." Okay, there's some crazy stuff in the Bible, but that sounds *insane*. How can we consider it a joy when we go through trials? That's literally the exact opposite of what we're hardwired to do!

If we keep reading, we can start to see why James—and the Holy Spirit through James—tells us to consider it a joy when we face trials because trials produce endurance, and endurance helps us become mature and complete Christians.

Nothing happens to you by accident. There were several seasons in my life that were not enjoyable at the moment: not being named a starter my freshman year at Houston, tearing my ACL my senior year, not getting drafted, being cut three times. But all of them happened under the control of God and for a reason. God's plans for us, ultimately, aren't about winning Super Bowls or getting drafted. They're not about the exterior, but about the interior—about making us more like Jesus. So whatever the exterior circumstances are, God is using them to make us into the person He wants us to be. That's why we can rejoice in trials.

What trials are you going through right now? A difficult marriage? A physical or mental sickness? Struggles with your friends or family members? A hard time at school? You don't have to enjoy the trials themselves, but you can have joy in the midst of the trials. Why? Because you can trust that God, who is in control of all things, is using those trials to accomplish His ultimate purpose in your life: making you more like His Son, Jesus.

Use the space below to respond to God
by writing a prayer to Him.

_____

_____

_____

_____

_____

_____

_____

_____

_____

_____

_____

_____

_____

_____

_____

_____

_____

_____

_____

_____

1 Thessalonians 5:16-18

Rejoice always, give thanks in everything; for this is God's will for you in Christ Jesus, pray constantly.

Day 19

Any Thanksgiving Day football fans here?

Like so many Americans, football was always a big part of our family's Thanksgiving traditions. Growing up in Texas, I always pulled for the Cowboys and their star quarterback, Troy Aikman. So naturally, when I got to start for the Vikings on Thanksgiving Day, helped the team win 30–24, *and* got interviewed by Troy Aikman himself after the game . . . it was a good day!

Thanksgiving is that one day a year when we all remember to be thankful. We give thanks for our families, our friends, our health, and all the other blessings God has given us. And when you're being interviewed after a win by one of your childhood heroes, it's pretty easy to be thankful. But the Bible tells us to be thankful not just in the good moments, but in all moments.

I don't know about you, but that's pretty tough for me! How am I supposed to be thankful after a blowout loss? After getting cut? After going undrafted? After tearing my ACL my senior season against UCLA? How am I supposed to be thankful when a tragedy touches my family, or in a difficult season of marriage, or when a friend lets me down?

I think this passage from the Bible gives us a hint. "Rejoice always, pray constantly, give thanks in everything." What do these three things have in common? They all come from a heart that is focused on God.

When we're focused on God, we'll always be rejoicing, even in the difficult moments, because we know how much He loves us and what He has done for us in His Son, Jesus.

When we're focused on God, we'll always be praying, because we know that He hears our prayers and that He is powerful enough to answer every single one of them.

And when we're focused on God, we'll always be giving thanks, even in hard seasons—not because of the difficult, but because we know He will use even that difficulty for our good.

So keep watching football on Thanksgiving, and keep giving thanks on that one fun day a year when you eat turkey, watch football, and spend time with the people you love most. But go even further than that. Spend every day thanking God for all the ways He has blessed you, and for the love He has for you.

Use the space below to respond to God
by writing a prayer to Him.

1 Thessalonians 2:8

We cared so much for you that we were pleased to share with you not only the gospel of God but also our own lives, because you had become dear to us.

Day 20

One of the best seasons of my life was the time I spent in St. Louis. It was short and sweet. Though we weren't there for long, Kimberly and I made some of our best friends.

We lived in a tiny apartment in St. Charles. Right down the hall from us? Offensive lineman Barrett Jones and tight end Brad Smelley—my best friends from the team. It felt like being in college in the dorm all over again. Late night *FIFA* games, epic board game battles, and never-ending games of Spades . . . we had a blast together.

And Kimberly was the best. Not surprisingly, she took great care of us. She cooked us big dinners, helped settle arguments (those *FIFA* games got competitive), and was always trying to help the other guys sort through their love lives.

Part of the reason this was such a fun season, I think, is that it was a cool picture of what the apostle Paul describes in 1 Thessalonians. When he and other missionaries first went to Thessalonica, they went to share the gospel with the people who lived there. But they didn't only share the gospel. Paul says, "We cared so much for you that we were pleased to share . . . our own lives."

This is a great example for us in two ways. First, Paul knew that the message of the gospel would seem less significant and be less effective among the Thessalonians if it wasn't packaged in love and friendship. The best way to share the gospel with someone is to do so in the context of a relationship. If you've shared your life with someone, if they know you care about them, then they'll be much more willing to hear you. People don't care what you know until they know you care!

Second, this reminds us of the importance of living in community with good friends and family. Who are you sharing your life with? Who is sharing their life with you? Are there people you love who you can count on, and who can count on you, no matter the circumstance or situation?

I knew when we lived down the hall from my boys, I could always count on them. And they knew they could always count on me. Pray for God to give you great friendships like that.

Use the space below to respond to God
by writing a prayer to Him.

John 10:27

My sheep hear my voice, I know them, and they follow me.

Day 21

I've had the chance to play for some pretty great coaches in my day. In my time at the University of Houston, I had six coaches, either head coaches or coordinators, who at one point were (or still are) Division-I head coaches.

One of the most gutsy play-callers I ever had was Kliff Kingsbury. Kingsbury came to Houston when Kevin Sumlin was our coach. He's known for his up-tempo offense—the guy likes to have a little fun on the field. A play-caller like Kingsbury makes some people nervous. Can they really trust somebody who is that gutsy? But we knew Coach, and we trusted him. As a quarterback, I had seen his play calls come through enough times to know I could trust him.

Jesus relates to us, in some ways, like a coach. Now, don't get me wrong—Jesus is much more than that. No coach will ever die to save you from your sins! But Jesus does give us instructions about how to live and how to follow him. Similar to a coach calling out plays and giving his players the responsibility to run them, Jesus speaks to us through His Word—the ultimate playbook—to teach us how to execute our lives in a way that is pleasing to Him. He speaks to us through His Word like a shepherd to his sheep—guiding us, leading us, caring for us, providing for us, and pointing us always in the right direction.

Just like I had to trust Kingsbury to run some of the plays he called, we have to develop trust with Jesus. He says His sheep know His voice. How can we get to know His voice? By spending more and more time listening to it. The more time we spend in God's Word, the Bible, the more we'll recognize Him as He leads us. The more we recognize Him as He leads us, the more we'll trust Him. And the more we trust Him, the more willing we'll be to obey Him—even when He calls us to do very difficult things.

Do you recognize the voice of Jesus? Are you following Him like a football player follows his coach, or a sheep follows a shepherd? Get to know Jesus, the ultimate coach, the Good Shepherd.

Use the space below to respond to God
by writing a prayer to Him.

_____

_____

_____

_____

_____

_____

_____

_____

_____

_____

_____

_____

_____

_____

_____

_____

_____

_____

_____

_____

Matthew 11:28

Come to me, all of you who are weary and burdened, and I will give you rest.

Day 22

Playing in the NFL takes a toll on you physically. I can see it when I hang out with former players. NFL training facilities are built to help counteract the wear and tear of the game as much as possible. Hot tubs, cold tubs, foam rollers, training, massage tables . . . all of these are meant to help you recover after a tiring game. And these are super helpful. But the thing is, the best you can hope for is to be back to 100 percent (or later in the season, back to 80 or 90 percent) by the next Sunday's game. Then you're just going to be exhausted again and go through the same routine!

But Jesus offers us rest and recovery that won't have to be replenished every single week.

Life in the world is tiring. Work, relationships, school, marriage, parenting, staying healthy, balancing finances—all of this is exhausting. And Jesus knows that, in addition to all of this, it's like we're hardwired to try to earn God's approval. We try to be good enough, to read our Bibles enough, to not commit certain sins . . . all in an attempt to impress God. But Jesus comes to us and invites us to rest. He tells us that the pressure is off; we can stop exhausting ourselves by trying to impress God, because God has already shown us how much He loves us by sending His Son.

That's why Jesus says in Matthew 11:28, "Come to me, all of you who are weary and burdened, and I will give you rest." The writer of the New Testament letter called Hebrews puts it this way: "For the person who has entered his rest has rested from his own works" (Hebrews 4:10). Jesus did all the work for us. We have fallen short in every way, and trying to be good enough to impress God will only leave us exhausted. But Jesus was good enough. He lived a perfect life, and He tells us that if we come to Him and believe in Him, His perfect life will count in our place. It's kind of like having an empty bank account. We all have empty bank accounts because we can't be good enough to please God. But Jesus has a full bank account. And when we believe in Him, God counts His bank account to ours—He gives us an unlimited line of credit. When we have this, we can rest! Why? Because we know that Jesus did all the work necessary to make us right with God.

Are you resting in Jesus? Have you come to Him yet? Or are you still weary and burdened, trying to be good enough to impress God? Take your weariness to Jesus. He will give you a light and easy load.

Use the space below to respond to God
by writing a prayer to Him.

_____

_____

_____

_____

_____

_____

_____

_____

_____

_____

_____

_____

_____

_____

_____

_____

_____

_____

_____

_____

Proverbs 22:1

A good name is to be chosen over great wealth; favor is better than silver and gold.

Day 23

My parents taught me a lot about integrity. First of all, they are good people themselves. Both my mom and my dad have a lot of integrity. They're always there for you. They stick to their word. And when we were growing up, they had very little tolerance for us doing otherwise.

For example, one thing you see a lot in college football recruiting today is that players will commit to a school, then de-commit and commit somewhere else—sometimes multiple times!—before signing day. Now, I don't want to be too hard on those kids; that's just the name of the game now. But that wouldn't have flown in Steve Keenum's house. When I got the offer to play for Houston and committed soon afterward, there was no de-committing and recommitting. It was as good as done. I was going to have integrity and be a man of my word and do what I said I was going to do, because that's what my dad and mom had raised me to do.

One reason it's so important to have integrity is because a good name is one of the most important things in life. What do people say when they hear your name? What kind of reputation do you have? Are you known for doing the right things, or for taking shortcuts? Are you a person of your word, or do you flake out? Do you go the extra mile, or do you take shortcuts?

The Bible says that a good name is so important that it "is to be chosen over great wealth." Having a reputation for being an honorable person, a person of integrity, is better than having a ton of money! Why? For a few reasons at least. Because money can come and go. Because you can have all the money in the world, but if you have no one to enjoy it with, it's no good. Because if you have a good name, people will have your back, but money can't buy loyalty.

The list could go on and on, but you get the point. Do the best you can to have a good reputation. And not in a fake way. Some people manufacture a good reputation, even though they're not great people. They just put on a show on the outside. But the best way to get a good name is to be kind, to have integrity, to be a person of your word, and, like Jesus says, to do for others what you would have them do for you.

Use the space below to respond to God
by writing a prayer to Him.

_____

_____

_____

_____

_____

_____

_____

_____

_____

_____

_____

_____

_____

_____

_____

_____

_____

_____

_____

_____

_____

_____

Psalm 100:1-5

Let the whole earth shout triumphantly to the Lord! Serve the LORD with gladness; come before him with joyful songs. Acknowledge that the LORD is God. He made us, and we are his—his people, the sheep of his pasture. Enter his gates with thanksgiving and his courts with praise. Give thanks to him and bless his name. For the LORD is good, and his faithful love endures forever; his faithfulness, through all generations.

Day 24

It's hard to succeed in life without goals. The old saying goes, "If you fail to plan, you plan to fail." And that certainly seems true to me. Before each season, football players and teams set goals: to win the Super Bowl, to make the playoffs, to throw thirty touchdowns, to pass for 4,000 yards, etc. We even set goals and make game plans before each game. For example, we may know in a certain game that if we can win the running battle and control the time of possession, we'll almost certainly win, so we'll build our game plan and goals around that.

The Bible says that God has a goal—for the world to know Him and for all the nations of the world to praise Him. Habakkuk 2:14 puts it this way: "For the earth will be filled with the knowledge of the LORD's glory, as the water covers the sea."

This was the goal when God originally created the earth. He told Adam and Eve to fill the earth with His image and His glory. Then after Jesus had been raised from the dead, He told His disciples virtually the same thing: "Make disciples of all nations."

This has always been God's goal, from the very beginning of creation. Psalm 100, which you just read, says it well: "Let the whole earth shout triumphantly to God!"

Why should we shout triumphantly to God? Why should we "serve the LORD with gladness"? Because He is good, "and his faithful love endures forever."

Can you imagine if the whole world really did give thanks to God in this way? Can you picture it? What would life be like if the whole world recognized God's love and faithfulness and gave thanks to Him constantly? Wouldn't the world be such a better place?

If this is what we want to see in the world, we should start with ourselves. I can help come up with the game plan for my team to reach our goals, but if I don't do my part, I'm not very helpful. I can call the plays in the huddle, but if I'm not paying attention when the ball is snapped, or if I throw the ball to the defense, or if I let the play clock run out and we get a delay of game penalty, I'm not very helpful at all! The same is true for us. We can recognize how good God's game plan is, but we have to do our part to fill the earth with His praise. This starts with us praising Him ourselves, and telling our friends and family about how great He really is.

Use the space below to respond to God
by writing a prayer to Him.

Matthew 28:18-20

Jesus came near and said to them, "All authority has been given to me in heaven and on earth. Go, therefore, and make disciples of all nations, baptizing them in the name of the Father and of the Son and of the Holy Spirit, teaching them to observe everything I have commanded you. And remember, I am with you always, to the end of the age.

Day 25

What's your purpose on Earth? Why are you here? What is life all about anyway?

OK, we are starting the day off with some pretty big questions. But have you ever really stopped to think about it? I mean, every person is just one of billions, and in one hundred years, probably nobody is going to remember you or me. So what is the point of it all?

When I was playing for the St. Louis Rams (back before the Rams moved to Los Angeles), Kimberly and I were introduced to a couple who helped us see more clearly the purpose of our lives. Jon and Tracy Sullivan were friends of a friend, and as soon as we met them, they brought us into their lives. They started "discipling" us.

Now, if you don't know what that means, don't worry—neither does my computer (it always shows up with one of those red lines under it). To disciple somebody is just to help them out as they are learning more and more what it means to follow Jesus. In the Bible, following Jesus is called *discipleship*. So discipling somebody is just helping them in their discipleship.

This is what Jon and Tracy did for us. Jon was always with me and some other bros walking us through God's

Word, teaching us what it meant, and challenging us to apply it to our lives.

Tracy did the same for Kimberly. She welcomed Kimberly into her home, read the Bible with her, and prayed with her.

Kimberly and I were Christians before then, but I think our view was a little too focused on ourselves. We knew that we were supposed to be like Jesus, but we didn't understand that, according to Jesus, the reason we're on this earth is to help disciple other people. Jon and Tracy showed us what this looked like—their lives are totally about making disciples.

Jesus makes this pretty clear too. Whenever I hang up the phone with Kimberly, the last thing I usually say is, "I love you." And that's the most important thing I say. If we don't listen to anything else someone says, we should listen to the last thing they say. And the last thing Jesus said to His followers before He left Earth was, "Therefore go and make disciples." This is why we're here! This is my purpose in life, your purpose in life. Regardless of where we are, what our job is, what our family situation is, we are called to be discipling others.

So let me challenge you with two questions: Who is discipling you? And who are you discipling? Pray that God will help you find answers to those questions.

Use the space below to respond to God
by writing a prayer to Him.

_____

_____

_____

_____

_____

_____

_____

_____

_____

_____

_____

_____

_____

_____

_____

_____

_____

_____

_____

_____

_____

Mark 1:35

Very early in the morning, while it was still dark, he got up, went out, and made his way to a deserted place; and there he was praying.

Day 26

If you spend a lot of time around Christians, you may start to hear some of them talk about their "quiet time." They say things like, "I had a great quiet time this morning," or, "I've been struggling today because I skipped my quiet time." But . . . what in the world is a quiet time?

Do people just get up in the morning and sit in silence at their coffee table? Do they go outside and sit cross-legged and close their eyes? If I did these things, I think I'd fall right back asleep!

A daily quiet time is not just about sitting in silence, but about clearing your mind and your heart, and getting alone with God by reading His Word and praying.

My first year in the NFL wasn't easy. It was definitely not what I expected. And at times, I got really restless. My mind was always racing, I was pushing way too hard, and my heart was uneasy. I realized something was missing from my life: a daily quiet time.

I saw, with the help of some other guys who have shown me more about what it means to be a Christian, that even though there's no command in the Bible that "thou shalt have a quiet time," there are some great examples of people who did have this practice—King David in the

Old Testament, and Jesus in the New Testament. And I'd say that's pretty good company!

Now, it's part of my routine every morning to get to my team's facility a little bit early. I'll grab a cup of coffee, open my Bible, and spend just ten or twenty minutes taking in God's Word and telling Him what's on my heart. I find that when I do this, even though I've been pouring myself out day-after-day on the practice field, during games, and in my relationships, these times with the Lord fill me back up. They prepare me for anything and everything that's facing me on a given day or week. And even if I don't feel like I learned anything particularly life-changing on a given day, I know God uses this time to make me more like Jesus.

So what would a daily quiet time look like for you? Maybe, like Jesus, you need to get up really early and go be alone in a quiet place with your heavenly Father. Maybe it's on your lunch break at work. Maybe it's the last part of your day right before bed. Whatever scenario works best for you, let me encourage you to make this part of your life. It will be well worth it.

Use the space below to respond to God
by writing a prayer to Him.

_____

_____

_____

_____

_____

_____

_____

_____

_____

_____

_____

_____

_____

_____

_____

_____

_____

_____

_____

_____

Proverbs 27:6

The wounds of a friend are trustworthy, but the kisses of an enemy are excessive.

Day 27

One of my closest friends and mentors is a guy named Mikado Hinson. Mikado was the chaplain at Houston when I was in school there, and he knew my dad a bit. Whenever I needed help or advice of any sort, Mikado was always one of my go-to guys.

One of Mikado's favorite sayings is a paraphrase of the Proverb you just read. He always says, "Better are the wounds of a friend than many kisses of an enemy." This is so important, and I wish I could help everybody understand this.

When you're playing quarterback, all eyes are on you, and it's really easy to start performing just for the praise that you get. In high school, you're trying to be the most popular guy in school and get college coaches to call and offer you scholarships. In college, you're trying to win the starting job, get some name recognition, and prepare to hear your name called on draft day. In the NFL, same drill—get the starting job, keep the starting job, and read some nice tweets from your fans.

But the problem is, all of this praise really amounts to very little. Don't get me wrong—it's great when people encourage you, and there really are loyal fans out there. But in the world of sports—and in the world of life—if you live for people's praise, you'll be crushed when they turn around and say you're no good.

It's not that it's bad to be applauded for doing a good job. I actually think this is a good thing. It's just that this kind of applause doesn't really help you grow as a person. But you know what does help you grow? Tough love.

Better are the wounds of a friend . . . Sounds kind of intense, doesn't it? But I don't mean *literal* wounds. Seriously, nobody wants friends who beat them up! What this Proverb means, and what my guy Mikado means, is that we need people in our lives who cut straight. People who tell us the hard truth. People who don't pull any punches.

When I tore my ACL during my senior season at Houston, I went into a dark place of frustration and depression. But after a while, I was just keeping myself there. I kept pouting and feeling sorry for myself, and I needed to adjust my attitude. And guess who was there to call me out—that's right, Mikado.

I hope you have some people in your life who will tell you the truth. Not friends who are mean to you just for fun—that's not real friendship at all. But people who will be honest with you for your good. That's what we need. That's how we grow.

Use the space below to respond to God
by writing a prayer to Him.

_____

_____

_____

_____

_____

_____

_____

_____

_____

_____

_____

_____

_____

_____

_____

_____

_____

_____

_____

_____

_____

_____

Ephesians 2:8-10

For you are saved by grace through faith, and this is not from yourselves; it is God's gift—not from works, so that no one can boast. For we are his workmanship, created in Christ Jesus for good works, which God prepared ahead of time for us to do.

Day 28

In football, you're always being judged by one question: "What have you done for me lately?" It doesn't matter if you broke every NCAA passing record imaginable yesterday, people judge you on today.

Take, for example, my experience at the NFL combine. Not my best day ever. You show up to run some drills and take some measurements in front of coaches from every NFL team. One of the drills most people know about is the 40-yard dash. Pretty simple—you run 40 yards.

Unfortunately, when I lined up for the 40, I looked up and realized who was going to be running right in front of me: Robert Griffin III. This dude was like the fastest quarterback in years. In fact, right before I step up to run, he nails a 4.41—the fastest 40 time for a quarterback in NFL history.

How did I fare? Well, a 4.79 on my first try . . . and a pulled hamstring on my second. Ugh. I finished the combine that day with a tweaked hamstring, and you can imagine how helpful that was on the other drills.

I guess you could say that football is a works-based religion. People show their love and acceptance of you based on your works. "What have you done for me lately?"

But Christianity is a grace-based religion. This is the amazing thing about Christianity. God doesn't look at us and ask, "What have you done for me lately?" He looks at us, poor and helpless as we are, and says, "Look what My Son did for you. That's how you know I love you. And all you do to have My full acceptance is believe in Him."

Now, that doesn't mean that once we're accepted by God, we can do whatever we want! If you keep reading to verse 10 of Ephesians 2, you see that He has prepared ahead of time good works for us to do. Loving your spouse. Respecting your parents. Getting involved in a church. Serving the poor. Praying for sick friends. Working hard at your job or your schoolwork. In Christianity, we're not saved by works, but we are saved *for* works.

So exhale. Know that God is not like an NFL coach. He doesn't accept you only if you're good enough; He accepts you because His Son Jesus is good enough. All you have to do is believe.

Use the space below to respond to God
by writing a prayer to Him.

_____

_____

_____

_____

_____

_____

_____

_____

_____

_____

_____

_____

_____

_____

_____

_____

_____

_____

_____

Galatians 1:10

For am I now trying to persuade people, or God? Or am I striving to please people? If I were still trying to please people, I would not be a servant of Christ.

Day 29

For most football players, draft day is *that* day. It's the day we grow up dreaming about. We visualize hundreds, thousands of times what it will be like to hear our name called, to shake the commissioner's hand, to immediately win the hearts of millions of fans.

For many of us, draft day is a disappointment.

I spent the months before the draft working my tail off, getting stronger, faster, more accurate. It was all for the purpose of being able to answer the questions, *Who will draft me? When will I hear my name called? What city am I moving to?* Unfortunately (well, it seemed unfortunate at the time), I went undrafted.

At times in my life, I've lived for the approval and applause of people. You can imagine how living for that approval and applause, combined with not getting drafted, made for a pretty rough day.

But the gospel—the good news of what Jesus has done to save sinners—totally flips that on its head. The gospel tells us that the approval of people does not ultimately matter. What matters is God's approval.

Whose approval are you seeking? Your wife's? That girl in second hour? Your coach? Your parents? Your teachers?

Can I let you in on a little secret? There will always be somebody you can't please. If you live for the acceptance and approval of people, there will always be one person who you can't win over, and it will crush you.

The good news is this: If you believe in Jesus and accept Him as Lord, then just as Jesus has God's approval, you have God's approval. You may want to read that again.

There's no need to spend your life working for the applause of people. At best, it's kind of useless; at worst, it will crush your soul. Rest in the approval of God. If you have faith in Jesus, it's already yours.

Use the space below to respond to God
by writing a prayer to Him.

Matthew 16:24-26

Then Jesus said to his disciples, "If anyone wants to follow after me, let him deny himself, take up his cross, and follow me. For whoever wants to save his life will lose it, but whoever loses his life because of me will find it. For what will it benefit someone if he gains the whole world yet loses his life? Or what will anyone give in exchange for his life?"

Day 30

The life of an NFL player can look pretty glamorous. In some ways, it is. We get to do what we love for a living. We do it on national television. People want our autographs. We travel on fancy planes and stay in nice hotels. It's a pretty pampered life, huh?

Now, don't get me wrong. We have to work really hard. I had to work really hard to get to where I am in the NFL, and I have to keep working just as hard to keep improving. It's not an easy life, even if it is glamorous.

A lot of kids grow up dreaming of that kind of lifestyle, and a lot of adults envy. But have you ever stopped and asked, *What is it all for?* How many starting quarterbacks in the NFL can you name off the top of your head? How many can you name from twenty years ago? A hundred years from now, do you think people will still be playing football at all?

One hundred years from now, people won't still be talking about my NFL career. In all likelihood, my great-grandchildren won't even know my name. The only thing that will matter one hundred years from now is my relationship with God. Did I, by faith in Jesus, come into a saving relationship with God, or not?

Jesus reminds us of this in Matthew 16 by asking one challenging question: "What will it benefit someone if he gains the whole world yet loses his life?" What will it benefit someone if he is in the NFL, has the best career ever, makes all the money in the world, has the perfect family, and seemingly has the perfect life . . . but doesn't know Jesus? Nothing. That person won't gain a thing.

What are you seeking to gain more than anything else in life? Success? Fame? A promotion at work? A wife? Children? Graduating from high school or college? Making a lot of money?

Let me challenge you—seek one thing above everything else. Even if you get everything you've ever dreamed of, it won't be worth it unless you have Jesus. One hundred years from now, that will be the only thing that matters about you.

Use the space below to respond to God
by writing a prayer to Him.

Conclusion

At the end of every season, whether in victory or defeat, every team will have to answer the question, "What's next?"

Some players will disappear into comfort. They will avoid getting back into their training regime. They might escape on expensive trips, not necessarily to rest and relax, but to procrastinate the kind of preparation required to win a Super Bowl.

Other players are the opposite. They know exactly what's next. They define their goals and resume preparation. Hey, there's nothing wrong with celebrating or recovering after a long season, but we all know that the very best players are willing to discipline themselves in order to achieve the same goal that every other player desires.

So, it's time to ask yourself, at the end of 30 days, "What's next?"

I hope the answer isn't to take a vacation from time spent alone with God. Instead, I hope you will find another book like this one, or better yet, open your Bible each day. If you don't know where to start, I'd encourage you to start in the Gospel of John. John's Gospel is the story of Jesus' life, told from one of His follower's perspectives. It gives an account of everything Jesus did in His earthly life that God wants us to know. It will change your life.

We began with John 3:16 (yes, the very same John!). That verse says:

For God loved the world in this way: He gave his one and only Son, so that everyone who believes in him will not perish but have eternal life.

These words, written down thousands of years ago, are just as true now as they were back then. God loves you. He loved you enough to send His Son, Jesus, to die in your place. None of us are perfect—the Bible describes that truth as sin. We've all messed up; we've all sinned against God and each other. That's the bad news. The good news is that Jesus died the death we should have died for our sins, so that we could live forever with God, in His kingdom.

So, let's ask it again: *What's next?*

About the Author

Case Keenum has traveled one of the most unique paths of any NFL quarterback. Case received only one scholarship offer, from the University of Houston, and went undrafted despite breaking multiple NCAA football passing records. He has overcome every obstacle to become a successful starting quarterback. In 2017, Keenum captured America's imagination by leading the Minnesota Vikings to a 13–3 record and an NFC North title. His game-winning touchdown in the final seconds of their divisional playoff game against the Saints, the "Minneapolis Miracle," made Case part of NFL history.

Keenum holds the all-time college football mark for passing yards (19,217), touchdown passes (155), total touchdowns (178), and completions (1,546). He was Conference USA Freshman of the year in 2007, Conference USA Offensive Player of the Year in 2008, and Conference USA Most Valuable Player in 2009 and 2011. He is one of only two quarterbacks to win the Sammy Baugh Award for the nation's outstanding passer twice (2009 and 2011).

Keenum signed with the Houston Texans as an undrafted free agent in 2012. He has a record of 20–18 as an NFL starter with the Texans, Rams, and Vikings. He posted career-highs in passing yards and touchdowns with Minnesota in 2017 and signed with the Denver Broncos in March 2018.